TIME TO LEARN ABOUT
WEEKS & MONTHS

Pam Scheunemann

Consulting Editor, Diane Craig, M.A./Reading Specialist

Published by ABDO Publishing Company, 8000 West 78th Street, Edina, Minnesota 55439.

Editor: Pam Price
Content Developer: Nancy Tuminelly
Cover and Interior Design and Production: Mighty Media
Photo Credits: JupiterImages Corporation, ShutterStock

Library of Congress Cataloging-in-Publication Data

Scheunemann, Pam, 1955-
 Time to learn about weeks & months / Pam Scheunemann.
     p. cm. -- (Time)
 ISBN 978-1-60453-020-9
 1. Time--Juvenile literature. 2. Week--Juvenile literature. 3. Months--Juvenile literature. 4. Calendar--Juvenile literature. I. Title. II. Title: Time to learn about weeks and months.
 QB209.5.S345 2008
 529'.2--dc22

                                    2007030079

$13.95

SandCastle™ Level: Transitional

SandCastle™ books are created by a team of professional educators, reading specialists, and content developers around five essential components—phonemic awareness, phonics, vocabulary, text comprehension, and fluency—to assist young readers as they develop reading skills and strategies and increase their general knowledge. All books are written, reviewed, and leveled for guided reading, early reading intervention, and Accelerated Reader® programs for use in shared, guided, and independent reading and writing activities to support a balanced approach to literacy instruction. The SandCastle™ series has four levels that correspond to early literacy development. The levels are provided to help teachers and parents select appropriate books for young readers.

Emerging Readers
(no flags)

Beginning Readers
(1 flag)

Transitional Readers
(2 flags)

Fluent Readers
(3 flags)

SandCastle™ would like to hear from you. Please send us your comments and suggestions.
sandcastle@abdopublishing.com

time

Time is an interesting thing. You can't touch it. You can't see it. You can't hold it. But it is always passing by!

Let's learn about measuring time in weeks and months.

time

The seven days of the week are Sunday, Monday, Tuesday, Wednesday, Thursday, Friday, and Saturday. These days repeat each week in this order.

We use calendars to track the days, weeks, and months.

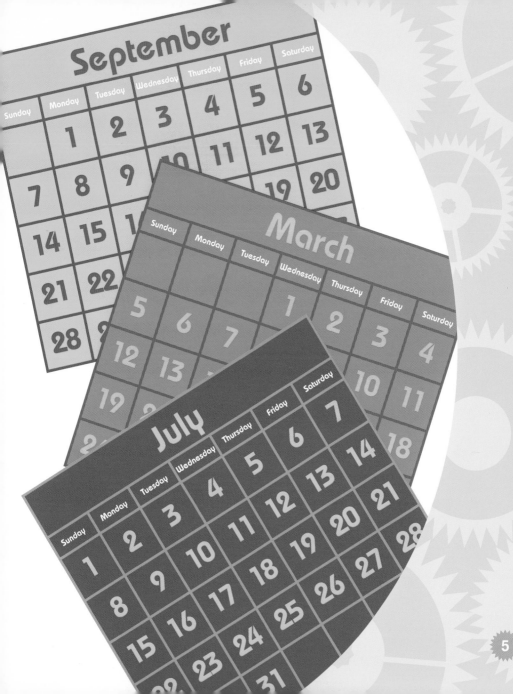

Marcus goes to school each weekday. He has art on Mondays. It is his favorite class.

The weekdays are Monday, Tuesday, Wednesday, Thursday, and Friday. Monday is named for the moon.

Tam has piano lessons each week on Wednesday afternoon.

Wednesday is the middle day of the week.

time fact

There is no school on the weekend. Dana likes to watch movies on Saturday nights. She likes weekends.

Saturday and Sunday are the weekend days.

time fact

For many people, Sunday is a day to relax. Gina enjoys spending time with her family on Sundays. They like to walk outside.

Sunday is the last day of the weekend. It is named for the sun.

A lunar month is how long it takes the moon to go around the earth. It takes about 29 and a half days.

The phases of the moon are caused by the changing angle between the Earth, the moon and the sun.

time fact

Kari uses this rhyme to remember the number of days in each month.

Thirty days has September,
April, June, and November.
February has twenty-eight alone.
All the rest have thirty-one,
Except in Leap Year, that's the time
When February's days are twenty-nine.

time fact

It takes one year for the earth to travel around the sun. The year is divided into 12 months. There are about 4 weeks in each month.

Linda and her family celebrate the Fourth of July, or Independence Day, every year. It is the birthday of the United States. Linda waves an American flag.

There are special days in each month throughout the year.

time fact

Mike brings flowers to his mom on Mother's Day. Mike wants to let her know that she is special to him.

In the United States, Mother's Day is always on the second Sunday in May. It falls on a different date each year.

One way to think about time is in terms of weeks and months.

What things do you do every week? Is there anything you do once a month?

time fact

Things we do once a week or once a month are done weekly or monthly.

What do you do on the same day each week?

What month is your birthday in?

In which months do you celebrate holidays?

Glossary

angle – the shape formed when two lines meet at a common point.

celebrate – to honor with special ceremonies or festivities.

certain – established or agreed upon.

favorite – someone or something that you like best.

orbit – to move in a circular path around something.

phase – a stage of the moon's changing appearance as it travels around the Earth.

To see a complete list of SandCastle™ books and other nonfiction titles from ABDO Publishing Company, visit www.abdopublishing.com.

8000 West 78th Street, Edina, MN 55439

800-800-1312 • 952-831-1632 fax